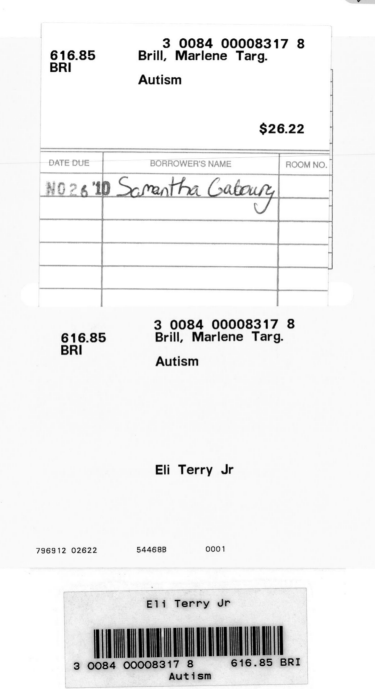

616.85
BRI

3 0084 00008317 8
Brill, Marlene Targ.

Autism

$26.22

DATE DUE	BORROWER'S NAME	ROOM NO.
NO 26 '10	Samantha Gaboury	

616.85
BRI

3 0084 00008317 8
Brill, Marlene Targ.

Autism

Eli Terry Jr

796912 02622   54468B   0001

Eli Terry Jr

3 0084 00008317 8   616.85 BRI
Autism

AUTISM

AUTISM

Marlene Targ Brill

Marshall Cavendish
Benchmark
New York

To families who live with autism, those who shared their stories, and readers who care enough to learn about this life-altering condition.

Marshall Cavendish Benchmark
99 White Plains Road
Tarrytown, New York 10591-9001
www.marshallcavendish.us

Library of Congress Cataloging-in-Publication Data

Brill, Marlene Targ.
  Autism / by Marlene Targ Brill.
      p. cm. -- (Health alert)
  Summary: "Discusses autism and its effects on people and society"--Provided by publisher.
  Includes bibliographical references and index.
  ISBN 978-0-7614-2700-1
  1. Autism--Juvenile literature. I. Title. II. Series.

  RC553.A88B75 2008
  616.85'882--dc22

                                    2007008786

Front cover: A child with autism
Title page: Chromosomes

Photo research by Candlepants Incorporated
Front cover: Ed Kashi / Corbis
The photographs in this book are used by permission and through the courtesy of: *Photo Researchers:* James Cavallini, 3, 28; Scott Camazine, 4; AJPhoto, 37; Jeremy Walker, 39; Nancy J. Pierce, 49, 54. *The Image Works:* Ellen B. Senisi, 9, 16, 20, 45, 52; Elizabeth Crews, 23; Johnny Crawford, 26; Bob Daemmrich, 48. *Corbis:* Tony Kurdzuk/Star Ledger, 15; Michael Macor/San Francisco Chronicle, 33; Steve Klaver/Star Ledger, 47. *Phototake USA:* Abrahame Menashe, Inc., 22, 24; ISM, 34. *Getty:* Lara Jo Regan, 56.

Printed in China
6 5 4 3 2

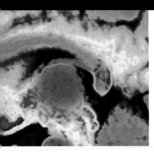

CONTENTS

1

WHAT IS IT LIKE TO HAVE AUTISM?

DAVID AND JAKE

David's life turned upside down after his baby brother, Jake, was born. Jake fussed all the time and cried around the clock. As Jake grew older, he never looked David or his parents in the eye. Jake would become very angry whenever David or his parents tried to cuddle him. Some sounds triggered tantrums.

At first, Jake babbled and eventually said *ba* for *ball* and *da* for dad, like other one-year-old kids did. Within six months, however, Jake stopped trying to talk. Instead, he imitated sounds of washing machines and other items with noisy motors and engines. He also giggled a lot while opening and closing doors to hear them slam. Jake stared at a single toy or repeated the same motion, such as flapping his hands, for hours. He liked to spin himself around and around. When not in motion, he liked to watch clothes swirl in the washing machine. Jake loved it when his mother drove over a highway, because he could look at cars speeding in rhythm along the road below.

In general, Jake seemed unaware of what was going on around him. But when he wanted something, he would holler until David reached for a particular toy or CD case on a high shelf. Even though he could not read, Jake knew which CD he wanted based on the label on its side. Jake behaved the same way when he attended a preschool program for children with special needs. But he never interacted with the other children.

At age five, Jake uttered as many sounds as an eighteen-month-old. His behavior was similar to that of a two-and-a-half-year-old child. He slept only a few hours each night. It was very difficult to keep up with Jake, and David and his parents were very tired. David pleaded with his mother and father to make Jake lie down and stop making noise, so they could sleep. Doors had to be locked, especially when every-one slept, or Jake would run outside. David's mother cried a lot and his father seemed sad.

David wanted more time with his parents, but they looked

so worried and tired all the time, that David never told them. He tried to be extra good at home and at school. David loved his brother and knew that Jake could not control what he was doing, but David often resented how much time and attention Jake was given.

Throughout the years, David's parents took Jake to different doctors. The first doctor said Jake was going through a childhood stage that he would outgrow. When the family worried about Jake not talking, the doctor told them to wait and see what would happen. Another doctor gave Jake medication that was so strong, Jake just sat still and stared into space.

Other doctors suggested putting Jake in an institution where he would live away from his family and be supervised twenty-four hours a day. Experts at the preschool claimed he would never learn anything.

David's parents decided to bring Jake to a school for children who had special needs. Staff at this school gave him tests and determined that he was autistic. This meant that Jake had problems with learning social and language skills. He might learn more slowly than other children, but no one knew for sure how much or how slowly.

Jake blossomed in the special school. A speech teacher helped him talk more and say the right words in the correct situation. Jake started speaking in sentences. At first, he echoed what people said to him or repeated commercials from television. As talking became easier for Jake, he repeated things less. He threw fewer tantrums since he could ask for what he wanted. Jake created an imaginary family and jabbered with them often. David's mother said this was Jake's way of blocking out a world that must be painful to him. She asked Jake to tell David stories about his pretend family at bedtime. David and Jake started connecting. They began having fun together, like other brothers do.

Jake learned so much at the special school that he transferred to a regular class at David's public school. A few hours a day, a teacher who understood autism came into Jake's class to help him organize his work and participate in group activities. A speech teacher continued activities to increase his language skills. Jake learned to read. He was able to do math problems easily in his head, which was good since his handwriting looked like chicken scratchings.

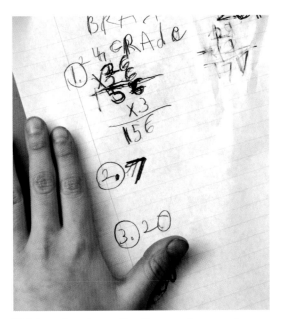

Writing clearly on the lines or in rows is often hard for many children with autism. As a result, their handwriting can be very dificult to read.

Teachers at the public school decided Jake had a **learning disability.** David's parents thought this was an improvement. The new label meant Jake could learn, just differently from other children. He still found social situations a problem, and when he talked he sometimes sounded like a computer robot. But there was no end to how much Jake could learn.

GRANT AND CARRIE

Carrie, on the other hand, worried about her younger brother's future. She and her parents first noticed Grant was different when he turned about ten months. He began banging his head on the floor and crib. He made no sounds except for screams. His crawling looked more like swimming. When he was one, Grant still could not stand, walk, or say any words.

Many doctors told Carrie's parents that Grant would just grow out of this stage, but Grant never did. He screamed at the grocery store and screamed if their mother stopped the car for gas. He played with the same object or stared into space for hours, screaming if anyone interrupted him. Grant did not say his first words until he was about four years old. He still ate baby food but put just about anything he could hold into his mouth. Rather than read, he ripped pages out of books and tried to eat them. Carrie had to keep her toys and books hidden or Grant would destroy them.

Grant eventually walked, but he kept in constant motion. He rocked on his knees while watching television or playing with a toy. Even when he stood in one place, he rocked from side to side. Carrie's parents put Grant's mattress on the floor so he could bounce and jump without hurting himself. When Carrie's mother read them stories at night, Carrie preferred to climb into her mother's lap while Grant ran in circles around the bedroom.

Grant's head banging continued. With time, he started banging his head into doors and windows. Carrie's father replaced the window in the front door so many times that he finally bought thick material for the window that would not break. Grant bit and scratched himself until cuts and wounds appeared over his legs and arms. The only activity that seemed to calm him was watching certain movies, which he started over and over again.

When he was five, Grant attended a new program for children who learned at a slower rate. He learned his ABCs and began to answer no instead of screaming. For conversation, he repeated phrases from cartoons. Two years later, he could spell his name and print some words, although he needed help remembering his phone number and address. It was still very difficult for Grant to sit in one place long enough to learn something new. He still disliked changing activities and preferred to do the same things over and over again. His teachers gave Carrie's parents little hope that much would change soon.

Carrie's parents joined a group with other parents of children who had autism. They all talked about their feelings and how they were handling their lives. However, Carrie mostly kept her thoughts to herself. She never told her parents how much she was teased for having a brother who acted differently. Even though she loved her family, she wished for a "normal" brother and a "normal" family. The whole family never went anywhere together. One parent always stayed with Grant because he caused so much trouble in public places. Either her mother or father took her to stores, restaurants, or family gatherings. Just once she wanted her whole family to go out together without tantrums.

Carrie eventually started talking to her guidance counselor—and later her parents—about how she was feeling. Talking about her feelings helped her handle things better.

Carrie hoped doctors would find a cure for autism one day. In the meantime, she and her parents studied everything they could to learn about autism and how to help Grant.

2

WHAT IS AUTISM?

Autism is a disability that affects how someone communicates and interacts with others. People with autism do not have an illness that comes and goes like the flu or a cold. Autism is not contagious, which means a person cannot catch autism from another person. The disability results from problems in the **nervous system,** which is made up of the brain, spinal cord, and a network of nerves that allow someone to move, think, and sense the world. How a person with autism learns and develops depends upon how the nervous system interacts with the environment around them.

UNDERSTANDING AUTISM

Children with autism usually appear physically normal, but they display a cluster or group of behaviors that are related to autism. Doctors identify autism by looking at a variety of signs that point to the condition and how it affects the way the person learns and develops. These signs can be mild or severe, depending upon the child. Every person is different.

Range of Abilities

The range of autistic behaviors is called **autism spectrum disorder.** At one end of the spectrum, or range, is **Asperger syndrome.**This is the mildest form of autism, so people who have it can function more independently. Unlike children who have severe autism, children with Asperger usually speak by age four. But the voice of a person with Asperger may sound flat and without emotion. Conversations may focus on concrete, straightforward topics or about one specific topic that greatly interests the child. In general, children with Asperger may have problems relating to or interacting with children their own age. Although children with Asperger syndrome may test well in regular school subjects, some may lack common sense and street smarts. Experts believe that Asperger syndrome is only one type of **high-functioning autism.** (In high-functioning autism, symptoms are less serious, which allows a person to behave in ways more similar to people without the disability.) Some believe Asperger syndrome is a separate condition from autism.

The addition of autism causes children with learning

The severity of a child's autism and his or her rate of learning can differ from child to child.

disabilities to experience and react to the world differently. More severe autism may interfere with learning and behavior enough to cause mental retardation. Retardation slows a child's ability to learn and progress. Results from studies differ in the number of children with autism who exhibit mental retardation. Part of the reason is children with autism vary widely in skills evaluated by standard tests. Some children do well on one part but not on another. Other children refuse to participate in testing situations, so their skills cannot be measured. Test results often change as children with autism gain new skills. Many believe that the important measure is not a test score but someone's continued ability to learn.

Certain autistic characteristics, such as poor eye contact, may remain in some form throughout a person's life. Others, such as tantrums, may change with time or fade completely. How much autism affects specific behaviors depends upon the individual child. For example, a combination of aging and training can help a person with autism lose many autistic behaviors. Improved social and communication skills can allow someone to focus better. In other cases, a person with

Most children with autism need one-on-one help and tutoring to make the most of their schooling.

autism may always have autistic traits that interfere with his or her ability to receive and relate information or to interact with others.

Senses in Autism

Many children with autism have problems processing information through their senses. They hear, feel, or see either too much or too little incoming information. This causes them to underreact or overreact to their environment. Children with autism may withdraw and become silent or unresponsive or throw tantrums to block out disturbing smells, sounds, touches, sights, or movements. They may scream to drown out sounds that are painful to them. They may also refuse to touch or eat items made of certain textures. These responses can be difficult for onlookers to understand. Such extreme responses can cause children with autism to miss **cues**, or clues, and important interactions that are a part of healthy development.

Progress with Autism

Children with autism rarely develop in the same pattern as others who are not autistic. Challenges related to autism affect the child's ability to achieve steady progress. Children with autism may take longer to reach common childhood milestones, such as walking, talking, or learning the alphabet. Or autism may cause normal progress to stop. Some babies with autism return to a younger stage or lose a skill entirely, such as no longer being able to talk.

SIGNS OF AUTISM

Although all areas of growth and development can be affected, the ability to communicate or be social are the most commonly altered skills. The following includes some common symptoms—or signs—of autism. Not all people with autism display every sign. A medical team with parent input diagnoses, or determines, whether or not a person has autism.

Early Signs

A few parents may notice differences in their baby. The baby may not want to eat, may never smile socially, or may look away when parents talk. All babies cry and scream but can usually be calmed down. However, babies with autism keep screaming and cannot be calmed easily. Washing, dressing, and cuddling a baby with autism can trigger battles that last long after the activity occurs. All babies are fussy at one time or another and may not want to be dressed or washed. But babies without autism usually learn to accept these changes or grow out of this fussy phase. In babies with autism, responding this way lasts longer than a phase that most kids outgrow.

Some babies with autism, however, do not respond to stimulus by screaming or fussing. Instead, they keep so quiet they never cry for food. As they age, they remain uninterested in their surroundings. They never reach for objects, explore their surroundings, or look at other people. Each type of baby with autism may display habits that seem odd. Babies with autism may rock, spin, bang their head, walk on their toes, or stare at their stiffly-held hands. Autism may cause them to form unusual attachments with objects or become overly sensitive to sounds or textures.

Communication

Babies with autism who make normal sounds, such as babbling or saying words, may stop talking between the ages of one and one and a half years. For some children with autism, their only communication becomes unexplained tantrums. Or they may communicate by pulling on somebody to reach a desired item for them.

Autism in older children results in a range of abilities to talk and understand what is heard. Some children appear deaf because they respond to sounds unevenly or not at all. They may remain mute throughout their lives, or they develop language as late as nine years old. Other children produce their own language. They may substitute words or letters to say what only they understand. When communication becomes understandable, children with

Communicating with others can be hard for children with autism. However, some are able to find common ground with other children their age.

autism may leave out words or letters when talking. Sometimes, they repeat words, phrases, or sentences after hearing them or they repeat them much later. Often, the repeated information does not relate to the conversation.

Children with autism who talk in regular sentences may have problems controlling the pitch and loudness of their voice. Their speech may have a flat tone. One hallmark of autistic language is the inability to handle back-and-forth conversations easily. This comes from being unable to pick up correct cues from their social world. People who have autism usually cannot tell from someone's tone or body language if the other person is kidding, serious, happy, or angry. Because they cannot understand these physical or verbal cues, the person with autism does not know how to respond in a way that fits the situation. As a result, the conversation may become awkward or filled with silent pauses. To fill the conversation voids, many people with autism will communicate by repeating commercials or songs.

Social Skills, Playing, and Behaving

Social problems separate autism from other disabilities. Many children with autism seem indifferent or uncaring toward other people. People with autism may make awkward attempts at interacting with others, or they avoid social situations completely. This lack of social skills can be one of the worst features of autism for families. Nothing hurts brothers, sisters, or parents more than children who cannot show or return affection. Children with autism may dislike displays of affection such as hugs, kisses, or pats on the back. They may

In classroom settings, children with autism usually separate themselves from their classmates.

overreact or underreact in response. Onlookers who do not understand the disorder may find the inability to relate to other people and situations embarrassing and unsettling.

Another key trait of autism involves behavior toward objects and situations. For example, children with autism play differently, most often without imagination. Some children with autism become uncommonly attached to a block or straw, or they spin a toy part for hours. They crave sameness and display a strong need to repeat one activity.

Any attempt to break this routine triggers violent outbursts. Some children injure themselves with repeated rocking, head banging, hand biting, or continued scratching or rubbing. Such extreme focus on an object, one detail of an object, or repeated behaviors may be the children's way to block out something that bothers them in the environment.

As children with autism age, this need to repeat motions and focus on items changes. Children may spend hours lining up cars a special way instead of more realistic pretend play. They may develop an intense interest in one topic, such as train schedules or memorizing names or numbers. Routines may take on new meaning. Mealtimes, preparing for school, or going shopping follow an exact process that must be repeated. Any attempt to change results in an outburst.

Studies have shown that most tantrums and the need for strict routines lessen by teenage years. Afterward, only a

Children with autism can spend hours doing a single activity that catches their interest.

Some schools have special classes where autistic students are given guidance on how to interact with children their age.

small percentage of people with autism continue to react with violent tantrums. Even the most advanced teens with autism usually remain aloof or detached from others. They do not or cannot respond to the people and situations around them. They have difficulty picking up cues from social interactions. Improving behavior and learning social skills require specific teaching.

Inability to Judge Danger

Many children with autism exhibit deadened or numbed senses. Without the ability to sense their world, these children may show little fear of real danger. For example, a reduced sense of touch may make them unable to understand that a stove is too hot to touch. Children who have no real sense of danger cannot judge whether or not a step is too high to leap from or why jumping into a pool without learning to swim can be a problem.

Seizures

One in four children with autism develop seizures. These occur when there is a sudden electric charge in the brain that causes a loss of awareness. Seizures produce a range of problems. The most severe problems are blackouts, which occur when a person loses consciousness, and convulsions, which are violent muscle shakes. Milder seizures involve unusual movements or staring spells. Seizures can begin when the child is a baby or a teen. Most seizures can be controlled with medication, and many children outgrow them. Seizures can also be a sign of different medical problems, so a proper diagnosis from a doctor is necessary whenever seizures appear.

Extraordinary Skills

Over the years, books, movies, and television shows have focused on people with autism who displayed amazing

This student with autism quickly solves a math equation. Though his autism may affect other areas of behavior and development, his math skills are far above the skills of other children his age.

abilities in one area. The most common talents involve drawing, mathematics, writing, computing, memory, music, and advanced reading. A person with autism might play piano without taking lessons or memorize pages from telephone books. These are called savant skills, and they provide some of the most confusing pieces in the autism puzzle.

Although interesting, most people with autism do not exhibit these skills. Only about one in ten children with autism develops an outstanding savant skill. Still, about one in two people with savant skills have autism. Many savants tend to lose their talent as their autism lessens. A small number of children are able to turn their savant skills into successful careers as adults. Most, however, never find avenues for their uncommon skills.

RARE OVERLAPPING CONDITIONS

Several other disorders share many of the same traits as autism. Children with autism can also be affected by one of the following disorders.

Rett Syndrome

Rett syndrome is a rare condition that mainly affects females. One of every ten thousand to fifteen thousand people gets Rett syndrome. With this disorder, a baby progresses normally at first. Between the ages of six and eighteen months, however, the child becomes disinterested in social contact and loses interest in producing sounds. In addition, children with Rett syndrome lose control of their feet and wring or squeeze their hands.

Scientists have uncovered a single **gene** that causes Rett syndrome. Genes are tiny parts of cells that determine characteristics and traits. Genes can also affect a person's development. Further study of the gene that causes Rett syndrome may give clues about how to slow or prevent the condition.

Fragile X Syndrome

Between 2 and 5 percent of autism cases are caused by Fragile X syndrome. This disorder mostly affects males. The name comes from a defect in the X **chromosome.** Chromosomes are the parts of a cell that carry the genes and information about

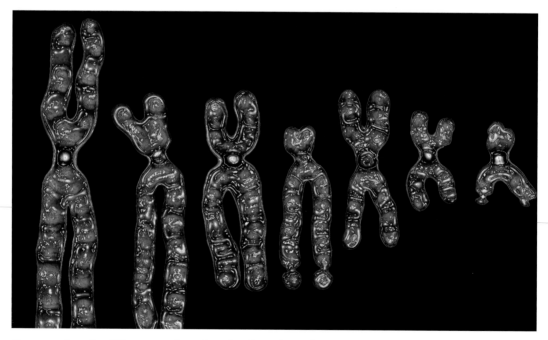

Progress in scientific research and technology has allowed scientists to examine human chromosomes. Understanding chromosomes can help with better diagnosis and treatment of many different diseases or disorders.

how a person develops. The abnormal X chromosome produces several physical changes, such as large ears and a long face. The syndrome also causes learning problems. Because Fragile X involves chromosomes, the condition can pass from parent to child. Fragile X is the most common form of inherited mental retardation. Signs of autism in Fragile X include anxious behavior and poor eye contact and speech.

WHO GETS AUTISM?

Autism can occur in any gender, race, ethnic group, or social or economic level. The disability touches every group around the world. For reasons that scientists cannot explain, autism affects boys more often than girls.

Autism is the most common disorder to alter development. According to a federal government study, around five out of every one thousand school-age children display autistic behavior. Individual states report numbers as high as nine out of every one thousand. These numbers total about 1.5 million individuals in the United States who have some form of the condition. Rates of new cases continue to climb by more than 10 to 15 percent each year. If these rates continue, in ten years the number of people in the United States with autism could climb to 4 million.

3

THE HISTORY OF AUTISM

Autism has been the subject of much interest and disagreement for decades. Until recently, few doctors thought of it as a separate condition. Doctors originally believed that autism was a part of other developmental disorders. The first documented report of the disorder now known as autism came in 1912 from Eugen Bleuler, a Swiss doctor. Dr. Bleuler noticed how certain adults withdrew from the outside world, rejected social contacts, and kept to themselves. He started using the term *autistic,* which stems from the Greek word *auto* meaning *self,* to describe these adults. Bleuler believed his patients showed a form of mental illness, rather than separate developmental problems.

The first description of autism as an individual disorder came in 1943. Dr. Leo Kanner used the term to describe a group of eight boys and three girls he observed from 1938 until 1943 at Baltimore's Johns Hopkins University. Kanner noticed that the children appeared bright although unaware of their environments. He wrote, "There is from the start an extreme autistic aloneness that, whenever possible, disregards, ignores, shuts out anything that comes to the child from the outside." He listed several problems with these children that he believed began in early childhood.

A year later, Viennese doctor Hans Asperger published a description of children who showed these and other behaviors. Since Asperger gave accounts of children with less disability, his name became associated with higher-level autism. Kanner and Asperger noticed that their patients were unable to show emotion or socialize. The two suggested that whatever this strange condition was, it must have been present since birth. At the time, this finding separated autism from mental illnesses that developed as people aged.

Kanner also noted that the parents of these autistic children were intelligent. He questioned whether these parents were so distracted with their own education and jobs that they acted preoccupied and disinterested toward their children at home. He wondered whether cold parents somehow contributed to their child's autistic condition.

OLD-FASHIONED THINKING

For the next twenty years, doctors explored child-rearing connections to autism. Bruno Bettelheim from the University of Chicago expanded upon Kanner's idea about bad parenting and its effect on disorders in children in his 1967 book, *The Empty Fortress.* Bettelheim was a **psychologist,** someone who studies the workings of the mind, emotions, and behavior. His research and writings called attention to "refrigerator mothers." Many believed these mothers were so cold and distant that their babies either refused to or could not bond with them. Bettelheim believed that this lack of bonding made the baby unable to thrive and interact with others.

His idea of treatment was to take children away from bad parents. He set up overnight schools and foster homes to house these children, but they proved to be unsuccessful. The children still had problems. This treatment, which blamed parents—especially mothers—needlessly tore apart many families.

During the 1960s, experts began to challenge the idea that autism stemmed from family problems or bad parenting. In 1964, Bernard Rimland, a psychologist and parent of a child with autism, proposed that autism resulted from a problem of biology rather than bad parenting. This meant that autism came from something the child was born with that could not be controlled or changed by his or her parents. By 1977, studies found a link between genes and autism. But change came slowly within the medical community. It was not until the 1990s before most doctors finally defined autism as a medical condition with specific signs and symptoms instead of a mental health problem.

MODERN RESEARCH

Recent studies point to different origins of autism, though the exact cause remains unknown. Today's research shows that several factors may contribute to autism. None of the possible causes include the concept of bad parenting.

Careful research proved that a person cannot develop autism as a result of having bad parents. Parental care, however, plays an important part in helping a child with autism develop and progress.

Brain Studies

Improved technology allows scientists to compare brains of people with and without autism. Pictures of the brain from a baby with autism show differences in structure and function. Some parts grow more rapidly while others remain underdeveloped. Special scans and images reveal that several parts of the brain are involved in autism. Two of the most studied parts of the brain are the cerebellum and limbic system. The cerebellum is a thin layer of gray folds that covers both halves of the brain. This layer controls high-level mental and movement activities and regulates attention, memory, and the senses.

The limbic system lies in the center of the

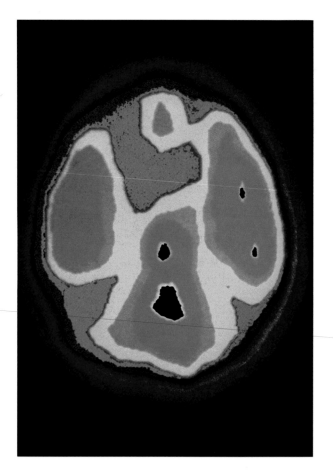

Special scans can help doctors examine the brain structure and brain activity of a person with autism.

brain. Its different parts govern emotions and behavior. Injury to the limbic system can change how children with autism relate to other people. Extreme emotions, such as crying or laughing at unusual times, unreasonable fears, sadness, or rages, can result. Studies continue to explore the brain as a source of autism differences.

Chemicals

Many researchers trace individual autistic behaviors in some children to an imbalance of certain chemicals or substances in the body. Children who display stomach problems together with autistic behavior may lack vitamin A. Vitamin A affects vision and the ability to focus with direct eye contact. One in two children with autism shows decreased vitamin B6. This vitamin helps with different types of cellular activity, which can affect development. Many children with autism have a decreased ability to feel pain because they lack other brain chemicals. Some treatment programs for children with autism recommend giving large doses of vitamins or other necessary body chemicals if the children have very low amounts in their bodies.

Doctors continue to study whether a link exists between certain food reactions and autism. One theory targets trouble in how the body absorbs gluten and casein. Gluten is a substance found in most grains, such as wheat, rye, and barley. Products made from these grains contain gluten. Casein is a substance found in dairy products. Parents and scientists concerned about gluten and casein believe that these substances enter the bloodstream and travel to the brain. Once there, they can alter brain activity and trigger signs of autism. As a result, some children with autism are on special diets that exclude products that include gluten and casein. Some feel that these special diets improve the children's behavior. However, any extreme changes in a child's diet should be approved by a medical professional to insure that the child has a healthy balance of vitamins and minerals. In the meantime, scientists continue to study whether or not vitamins, chemicals, and other similar substances affect autism.

Vaccines

One of the most hotly debated possible causes of autism involves **vaccines,** which are shots that prevent diseases and other illnesses. Disagreement developed after a London doctor named Andy Wakefield noticed that children with certain intestinal disorders seemed more likely to develop signs of autism after they received the combined shot to prevent measles, mumps, and rubella (MMR). His 1998 report covered only a few children, but it caused concern in the United States, which was experiencing a rise in autism cases. Besides the ingredients that protect against diseases, vaccines also contain certain chemicals that help preserve the vaccine. One of these chemicals is mercury, which can be toxic or poisonous. Scientists studied the number of vaccines a baby received and the amount of toxic substances used in the vaccines. They found that too much mercury in the body triggered many of the same behaviors as autism.

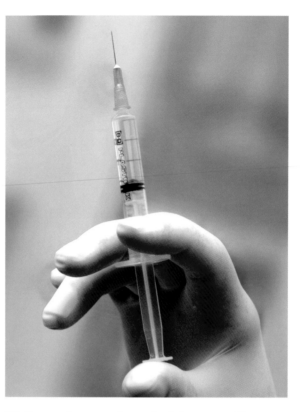

While vaccines are important for preventing illness and diseases, some of the chemicals in the vaccines could be dangerous.

The federal government responded by banning mercury in many vaccines and conducting more studies. But small amounts of a form of mercury still appear in lingering vaccines. Study results showed no relationship between MMR vaccines and autism. But the number of children who may have received mercury-laced vaccines was not counted in the study. Many doctors and scientists feel that it is more dangerous for children not to receive vaccines. They think that the seriousness of the diseases that the vaccines prevent far outweighs the problems that may or may not be caused by ingredients in the vaccines. Many parents who find high levels of mercury in their children's bloodstream do not agree. Today, studies for both sides continue.

Other Possible Causes

Several factors influence the health of children before and after they are born. Many, such as certain infections and bacteria, have been found to damage the nervous system. Researchers continue to search for links between autism and illnesses that strike mothers during pregnancy and children after they are born.

Another growing concern is the negative influence on the nervous system from toxins in the environment. Studies confirm that brain and other system damage results from being exposed to high levels of lead, mercury, and other chemicals. Clusters of autism have been found around the country. This means that there are many cases of autism in a particular area. Usually, these areas have unsafe levels of certain chemicals in the ground, air, and water. However, federal government tests show no link between problems with the

Some researchers believe that pollution from factories and chemical plants plays a role in causing autism in children.

environment and autism. But families who deal with autism and live near factories spilling dangerous chemicals remain unconvinced.

Many parents report fewer autistic signs after giving their child drugs that clean metals from the body. First, doctors test either the child's hair, urine, or blood. If any of these show high levels of metals, such as iron, lead, mercury, or zinc, the child receives daily doses of medication to remove the metals from the blood stream. The medication can be in pill, cream, powder, or liquid form. Three out of four families reported to the Autism Research Institute that they found this treatment helpful. Unfortunately, the medications can be dangerous and are expensive. Any kind of treatment needs to be supervised by a trained medical professional. And the federal government warns against jumping into this treatment before more studies offer concrete proof of the metal-autism link.

Family History

Researchers are exploring whether an error in one or more chromosomes causes autism. Humans have twenty-three pairs of chromosomes, which come from both parents. Each chromosome is made up of thousands of genes. Scientists estimate that there are 100,000 genes in the human body. Each gene tells body cells how to grow.

To investigate the role of genes, scientists collect blood samples from children with autism and their families. Studies suggest that autism results from several different genes. Gene research shows a 50 to 100 percent likelihood that autism will reoccur in the same family. Besides autism, families with autism report a 15 percent higher rate of brothers and sisters having other learning problems, such as severe learning disabilities. Among identical twins who share the same genes, the risk of both children having some type of language or learning problem skyrockets to 90 percent.

Gene studies raise as many questions as answers. How do genes explain traits that seem to result from other causes?

Some genes may not cause autism, but they could increase the likelihood that someone will develop autism if conditions in the environment trigger the disorder. Several organizations sponsor programs to interview families, test blood and cells, and prepare brain scans. The search for more definite answers to the autism riddle continues.

Autism Myths and Facts

Over the years, many false claims have been made about people with autism. Here are some of the most common:

MYTH: Children can never outgrow their autism.

FACT: Children with autism display a variety of signs. More often, some form of these traits persists throughout life. But characteristics of autism usually lessen with age and constant treatment. A small percentage of children with autism grow into independent adults.

MYTH: Children with autism cannot learn.

FACT: Autism may contribute to slower learning, sudden bursts of learning, and long lulls in between. But learning will occur.

MYTH: Children with autism can control their actions.

FACT: Autism is a medical condition. As such, people with autism react to their environment. They do not misbehave on purpose.

4

LIVING WITH AUTISM

Not long ago, doctors encouraged parents to place their children with autism in institutions. Today, the push is to keep children at home with their families and include them in community programs. We know that people with autism can improve, adjust, and live fulfilling lives.

Without an exact cause or cure, however, experts often disagree about the best course of treatment. Should children receive calming medicines, vitamins, or drugs to remove metals, or should they be on special diets? For some children, a combination of treatments works best. But any treatment plan must include education with behavior management to help individuals learn to function in the everyday world. Depending upon the community, a range of programs is available to treat children with autism and support their families.

IDENTIFYING AUTISM

The first step to treating autism is to make certain that the person actually has autism. Autism creates a range of behaviors. Many symptoms mimic or overlap other disabilities. Therefore, identifying the condition can be a long and difficult journey. Recent studies have resulted in a list of signs that enable doctors and parents to recognize babies at risk for autism. Without a single cause, however, much of the identification process relies on ruling out other conditions.

To identify autism, doctors depend on parents to provide clues about their child's activities at home. Parents must tell doctors about the family's medical history. A parent must also tell the doctor about milestones in the child's development. These include events such as saying some words by the age of twelve months and using two-word sentences by twenty-four months.

After taking a complete history, the doctor uses tests to rule out hearing, vision, and other nervous system problems. Some doctors order tests to take pictures or scans inside the brain or to check the pattern of electrical activity in the brain. If a child seems healthy based on these tests, the doctor then looks for behaviors that match the definition of autism listed in the American Psychiatric Association's *Diagnostic and Statistical Manual of Mental Disorders.* Doctors use this handbook to determine if a person has a mental disorder.

The doctor may recommend that parents take their child to a psychologist, a speech and language therapist, or an audiologist. The psychologist compares the child to development and behavior scales. These scales show how the child functions compared with other children of the same age. The speech and language therapist assesses hearing and speech and language difficulties. If the child fails to hear normal sounds, the audiologist uses special equipment and techniques to determine hearing loss. The combination of tests helps identify autism. Once a diagnosis of autism is made, families, doctors, and other health professionals agree on a course of treatment or therapy.

EARLY INTERVENTION

The first three years of life are key to how children learn and develop. Therefore, the most effective treatment to relieve signs of autism begins as early as possible. Babies with autism need structured programs to help parents improve their child's social and communication skills. These programs are called early intervention.

Federal law requires local public schools to provide early intervention services to all children 0 to 5 years who are disabled. With early intervention, someone from the program observes the child at home. The person watches how the child behaves and asks parents about sleep and bathroom habits, and any problems. The observer and parents agree on a treatment plan for the child based on the information collected.

Follow-up treatment occurs at home or in a clinic or classroom. Part of the program involves parents learning treatment methods to continue outside of the clinic or classroom. Parents meet people trained in **behavior modification,** speech and language therapy, and dealing with overdeveloped or underdeveloped senses.

Children with autism can receive help at home and in classroom settings.

Behavior Modification

According to the Autism Society of America, "Children with autism are not unruly kids who choose not to behave." Yet, behavior often makes life difficult for children with autism. They find relating to other people and suffering through social situations difficult. Their behavior poses the greatest challenges to family members. At home, facing frequent outbursts and constantly watching to prevent dangerous situations can be draining. In public, parents may feel others are judging their parenting of an unruly child. One way to lessen problems with autism is through behavior modification. This is the only method proven to consistently reduce autistic behaviors.

Behavior modification is a structured plan to change incorrect behaviors and learn new skills. Children with autism are often unsure of how to behave. With behavior modification, a parent, teacher, or therapist arranges conditions so the child can predict how to behave. Tasks are broken into smaller steps to make following them easier. Children with autism may work on looking at the teacher or imitating one sound or action. When these behaviors are repeated upon request, teachers reward the child with praise or small treats, such as a piece of cereal. Everyone likes to be rewarded. Rewarding

Sometimes teachers will introduce activities that can help children with autism relax and focus. This teacher is showing her students how to practice yoga.

positive behavior helps insure the same behavior will happen again. With time, the child learns to behave correctly.

Communication Aids

Communication remains one of the most important tools a person develops to interact with the world. Autism may limit use of that tool. Speech and language therapists work to improve the child's ability to communicate. They use simple sentences to explain what they want. They may apply behavior modification to teach someone how to follow directions.

They arrange activities that expand the number of words the child understands. Therapists also teach the child when and where to say certain words.

Computers are often used to help with communication skills. Some children with autism naturally take to computers as a means of communication. They can spell words on a letter keyboard beyond the ability of other children their age. Other

Using a combination of pictures, simple text, and the actual objects, teachers can help increase the vocabulary of a child with autism.

nontalkers prefer using a communication board. The board allows them to point to the words *yes* or *no,* or to pictures instead of talking.

Once children with autism gain enough language, they may

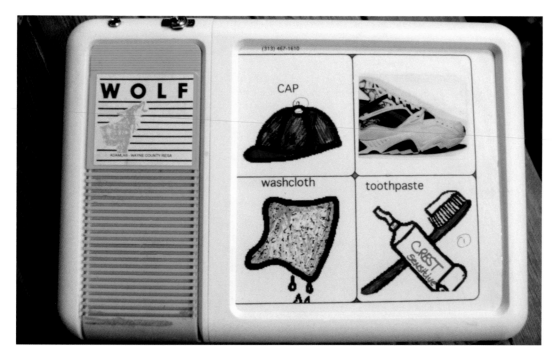

This communication aid helps an autistic person communicate with others. When he or she presses down on the item, the name of the object is played through the speakers.

benefit from learning through social stories. Teachers or parents relate stories about specific situations, such as riding the bus, avoiding things that are dangerous, or eating at a restaurant. The stories explain how different characters in the social setting relate to each other and what they say and do. This allows the person with autism to better understand what to expect and how to respond.

Calming the Senses

Many children with autism overreact or underreact to

information coming in through their senses. This may result in repeating or avoiding actions to block out hurtful sounds, sights, or feelings. Several methods help children deal with these sensations.

One method comes from **occupational therapists,** professionals who encourage daily life skills. Occupational therapists put the child through movements, such as spinning, swinging, and rolling. Such activities change how the body moves through space, which helps alter how the child sees and hears. The therapist may also rub the child's skin with different textures or apply pressure to different parts of the body. These activities improve the child's ability to handle touch and reduce the urge to pull away.

Children who find certain sounds painful may develop behavior, such as rocking or screaming, to block them out. One way to relieve the pain is to present the sound at a low pitch and gradually increase the sound level. This treatment retrains ears to adjust to hearing unpleasant sounds, so the child can learn to tolerate them.

Children who react to light find colored filters over glass lenses helpful. Reducing incoming light helps the child focus and improves attention. Children who react to touch may find wearing snug clothes or a weighted vest calming to the nervous system.

SCHOOL YEARS

At age five, children with autism move into programs beyond early intervention. Federal laws order public schools to educate children with disabilities through age twenty-one. Schools provide a range of options for children with autism based on their ability to progress. When a child enters school, educators and parents meet to decide on a plan for that child. This plan determines the type of school setting that will produce the best results. Sometimes, the plan includes recommendations for continuing speech and occupational therapy.

Some children with autism attend special schools. Others participate in neighborhood school classes. They may enter a special class for students with disabilities or a class with nondisabled students. To help them focus, students with autism may work alongside an aide or special education resource teacher.

Some students with autism may participate in a regular class for certain subjects and go to a resource room for other subjects or periods of the day. Teachers in resource rooms have special training in working with children with disabilities. They tailor subjects to individual student needs and provide support for the student with autism and the student's

This student wih autism uses a simple list to remind him of what he needs to do in class.

other teachers. Resource teachers may teach reading, writing, and math, but at a slower rate. Or they may emphasize daily living skills, such as creative play and making friends.

As students age, classes address more practical instruction. The focus may change toward job training and independent living skills. Social stories for older students may depict job interviews, chatting with coworkers, and using public transportation. Teachers may offer suggestions for free-time interests outside of school and work.

AFTERSCHOOL YEARS

Many adults who display few signs of autism or have Asperger syndrome eventually leave school to work and live independently. A small number attend college. Even with these successes, adults with autism may experience difficulties making friends and interacting with others. In these situations, they need continued support to remain independent.

At Work

More severe signs of autism require different levels of assistance to manage jobs and living arrangements. Federal, state, and local agencies offer a variety of choices based on individual skills and location. Someone with autism may need a job coach to support their work alongside nondisabled employees. Or they may participate in programs that concentrate on social skills, daily living, and recreation skills, or a sheltered workshop. In sheltered workshops, work activity centers, or adult daycare programs, the staff trains and supervises adults with disabilities to perform specific tasks. Usually, the jobs involve assembling piecework, such as in packaging, assembling, sewing, or stuffing envelopes. Instead of regular pay, as in nondisabled situations, workers receive small amounts for each item they complete. A few adults with savant skills transform their skills, as with computers, for example, into employment opportunities as adults.

At Home

Living arrangements for adults with autism depend upon similar abilities for self-care. Independent adults with autism live totally on their own. Semi-independent apartments allow residents to live and work on their own, but provide a staff person who checks in regularly. Adults who need added support can live in group homes shared with other individuals with disabilities. With group homes, the staff supervises

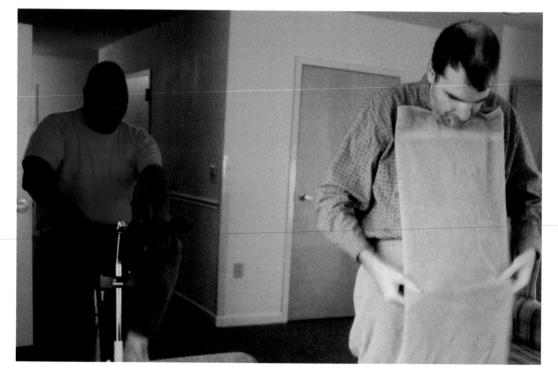

Some young and older adults with autism live in group homes, where they live with other people with autism.

everything from daily programs to recreation. They coordinate residents' travels to jobs, adult daycare, or other programs outside the home. Those who require constant supervision live in twenty-four-hour settings. These settings offer activities and shelter to adults who cannot take care of themselves.

BROTHERS AND SISTERS

Autism distorts the normal ups and downs between sisters and brothers. How can you fight with someone who erupts into unexpected odd behaviors? How do you play with some-one who refuses to communicate or gets lost in the same activity for hours? What can you do to attract attention of parents who may be constantly worried, upset, and exhausted?

Brothers and sisters display a range of reactions to autism, including guilt, rage, concern, and embarrassment. Some **siblings,** or brothers and sisters, feel they must try to be perfect because they are the healthy child. They take care not to say or do anything that will cause their parents more problems. Other siblings do poorly in school or act out to get attention from their parents. Each group may harbor hidden fears and feelings about having a sister or brother with autism.

Parents find different ways to address concerns of all family

Support and help from siblings can make a huge difference to children with autism.

members. Some families hold regular family meetings. At these meetings they talk about what autism is and how to deal with someone who responds differently. When talking together is difficult, several community groups help parents support their nondisabled children. Programs, such as the Sibling Support Group, offer support for siblings of children with disabilities. These groups provide a safe place to share feelings about living with someone who has autism. Some groups have activities just for siblings. That way, sisters and brothers can enjoy themselves without thinking about autism. These support groups may also help them come to terms with their family situation.

SHARING INFORMATION

Too many people with autism become the object of teasing or tormenting. Bullies encourage children with autism to do things that they do not recognize as wrong. Other children may ignore someone with autism for wrongly fearing they will catch the disability or be unable to interpret autistic reactions. Similarly, siblings may experience teasing about their unusual sister or brother.

Most teasing results from a lack of understanding. To counteract teasing, many families offer neighbors and schoolmates information about autism before problems occur. Parents may send teachers and program leaders written information before the child with autism arrives in class or summer camp. They may suggest a presentation to the class or group. During presentations, either a parent, child with autism, sibling, or combination of family members present facts and answer questions. They define autism and explain what life with the disability is like. They reinforce that children with autism are people first. And, like everyone else, people with autism have the same desire to be accepted and treated with respect.

Knowing the facts reduces fears of autism. As a result, classmates and neighborhood children may be more likely to include someone with autism in their activities. Bullies lose their power because they cannot attract an audience who accepts their teasing children with disabilities. In some classes, teachers assign a student to work alongside the person with autism. In others, the entire class shares the task of ensuring a classmate with autism participates in activities.

THE FUTURE

The goal for any parent is to raise happy, independent children. Parents harbor the same dream for their child with autism. With continued research, this dream may come true for everyone dealing with autism. Researchers are moving closer to identifying autism earlier and discovering one or more causes. Once causes and their triggers are confirmed, doctors can explore ways to prevent and eliminate the condition. But this will take time. In the meantime, people with autism continue to make great strides, entering programs with the nondisabled and taking their place in the community.

GLOSSARY

Asperger syndrome—The mildest form of autism. It usually affects social skills.

autism spectrum disorder—The range of autistic behaviors from mild to severe.

behavior modification—A structured plan to change incorrect behaviors and learn new skills by rewarding correct behaviors.

chromosomes—Small parts of a cell that carry genes and affect characteristics, traits, and development. Chromosomes are passed from a parent to a child.

cues—Signs or signals that help a person understand a situation or decide what to do. Cues may be verbal or physical.

fragile X syndrome—A rare condition from a defect in the X chromosome that causes physical changes, mental retardation, and signs of autism mostly in males.

genes—Tiny parts of cells that determine characteristics and traits.

high-functioning autism—A form of autism in which the symptoms are less serious, allowing a person with the disorder to behave in ways more similar to people without the disability.

learning disability—Learning differences that interfere with acquiring information.

nervous system—The brain, spine, and network of nerves that transmit messages to and from the brain to different parts of the body so that someone can move, think, and sense the world.

occupational therapist—A specially trained person who encourages daily life skills and works to reduce painful senses in people with autism.

psychologist—Someone who studies behaviors and mental problems related to the mind. A psychologist treats a person with these problems through counseling.

Rett syndrome—A rare condition passed through genes that affects mainly females. It causes babies to lose speech, social skills, and control of limbs at around the age of eighteen months.

seizure—A sudden electric charge in the brain that causes a range of problems in the body.

siblings—Sisters and brothers in the same family.

FIND OUT MORE

Organizations

Autism Society of America

7910 Woodmont Ave., Suite 300

Bethesda, MD 20814-3067

301-657-0881

http://www.autism-society.org

CAN (Cure Autism Now)

5455 Wilshire Boulevard, Suite 2250

Los Angeles, CA 90036

888-828-8476

http://www.canfoundation.org

Books

Chara, Kathleen. *Sensory Smarts: A Book for Kids with ADHD or Autism Spectrum Disorder Struggling with Sensory Integration Problems.* London, England: Jessica Kingsley Publishing, 2004.

Lennard-Brown, Sarah. *Autism.* Chicago: Raintree, 2004.

Meyer, Don. *The Sibling Slam Book: What It's Really Like to Have a Brother or Sister with Special Needs.* Bethesda, MD: Woodbine, 2005.

Web Sites

Autism Research Institute
http://www.autism.com

Best Buddies
http://www.bestbuddies.org

KidsHealth for Kids: Autism
http://www.kidshealth.org/kid/health_problems/brain/
  autism.html

Kids' Quest on Disability and Health: Autism
http://www.cdc.gov/ncbddd/kids/kautismpage.htm

Sibshops: Sibling Support Project
http://www.siblingsupport.org/sibshops/index_html

ABOUT THE AUTHOR

Marlene Targ Brill writes about many topics, from history and biographies to world peace and tooth fairies. Her favorite topics involve ways to help people understand each other better. Sharing information became part of her job when she taught children with special needs, particularly autism. For thirteen years, she worked to help students with and without disabilities understand that they were more alike than different. Now she writes about special needs, such as Down Syndrome, Tourette Syndrome, and autism in books for young readers. She also writes about special needs for adults, as in *Keys to Parenting a Child with Autism* and parts of *Raising Smart Kids for Dummies.* She lives near Chicago with her husband, Richard, and daughter, Alison.

INDEX